Thank You for Serving with a Heart like Jesus

Dr. Jane L. Fryar

Thank You for Serving with a Heart like Jesus

Dr. Jane L. Fryar

www.CTAinc.com
Copyright © 2003, 2007 CTA, Inc.
1625 Larkin Williams Rd.
Fenton, MO 63026-1205

ISBN 978-1-933234-50-2
Printed in Thailand

To

Deanna Miracle

From

Pastor Jerry Miracle

Thank you for serving
with a heart like Jesus!

*We give thanks to God always for you all,
making mention of you in our prayers;
Remembering without ceasing your work of faith,
and labour of love, and patience of hope
in our Lord Jesus Christ,
in the sight of God and our Father.*

1 Thessalonians 1:2–3 KJV

. . . the hearts you touched

. . . the wisdom you shared

. . . the love you showed

All of these reveal the ways the Lord Jesus
is at work in you, shaping and forming your
heart so that it conforms more
closely to the contours of his own.

The high delight of
serving Christ's people
belongs to those who first
admit their own need for
the Savior's forgiving,
healing touch.

We do not have a high priest who is unable to sympathize with our weaknesses, but we have one who has been tempted in every way, just as we are— yet was without sin.

Let us then approach the throne of grace with confidence, so that we may receive mercy and find grace to help us in our time of need.

Hebrews 4:15–16

*Whatever you do, work at it with
all your heart, as working for the Lord,
not for men, since you know that you
will receive an inheritance from the
Lord as a reward. It is the Lord
Christ you are serving.*

Colossians 3:23–24

The difference between
servitude and *servanthood*
is the difference between
have to and *get* to.

What motive stirs my service—
a "have to" or a "get to"?

_____

[Jesus said,] "I am the vine;
you are the branches. Whoever abides in me
and I in him, he it is that bears much fruit,
for apart from me you can do nothing."

John 15:5 ESV

_____

Thank You for Serving with a
Heart like Jesus

Jesus loved. And in love, he served.
That love led him all the way to the cross!

Jesus' followers, in turn, served him and
one another with hearts set ablaze by his love.

*What part of Christ's service
on my behalf touches me
most deeply?*

As the Father has loved me, so have I loved you.
Now remain in my love.

John 15:9

" . . . the Father himself loves you!"

John 16:27 ESV

Usually, the New Testament uses the word
agape to describe God's love toward us.
But here, Jesus uses the word implying
affection and friendship. The heavenly
Father's heart overflows with feelings
of friendship and fondness—for *you!*

[Jesus said,]
"I am among you as one who serves."

Luke 22:27

*God is not unjust; he will not forget
your work and the love you have
shown him as you have helped his
people and continue to help them.*

Hebrews 6:10

Lord God, Holy Spirit,
open our eyes to see Jesus'
love in all its splendor!
And may that love
inspire us to
serve more lovingly!

[Jesus] said to all, "If anyone would come after me,
let him deny himself and take up his cross daily
and follow me. For whoever would save his life
will lose it, but whoever loses his life for
my sake will save it."

Luke 9:23–24 ESV

Speaking the truth in love, we will in all things grow up into him who is the Head, that is, Christ.

Note that St. Paul calls for truth spoken in love,
not truth stripped of mercy or compassion.
Jesus' followers were able to hear
and apply the truth Jesus
spoke because they knew
he said what he said
not to hurt,
but to help.

18

O blessed Teacher, Holy Spirit,
continually encourage my heart in the
love our Savior has for me. And may I,
in turn, develop ever-deepening
courage and integrity so that I speak
the truth in love to those I serve
and those who serve with me!

John the Baptist tried to explain his relationship to Jesus, showing us what ours should also be:

He must increase, but I must decrease.

*But when the Helper comes,
whom I will send to you from the Father,
the Spirit of truth, who proceeds from
the Father, he will bear witness about me.
And you also will bear witness,
because you have been with me
from the beginning.*

John 15:26–27 ESV

O Holy Spirit, Comforter and Friend,
impress upon my heart the meaning of
Christ's service for me. And may I,
in turn, worship him as I humbly
serve his people!

In our Lord's hands, our
lives of service take shape.
As he works in us, we
become his work of art,
vessels uniquely suited
for specific purposes.

In important matters,
never settle for *good* ideas
until you've prayerfully
searched for *great* ideas!

What we do for Christ grows out of who we are in Christ.

The more closely our attitudes and
actions match our core identity
as Jesus' redeemed people,
the more authentic—
and genuinely helpful—
the service we render.

Heavenly Father, grant that I may submit gladly and willingly to the Spirit's gentle shaping of my heart so that my service flows ever more authentically from a heart like Christ's own heart!

The process of trying to control others
holds out an empty promise—
the promise of "power over."

True service, freely given, delivers the
"power to" create positive results that
benefit both giver and receiver.

Influencers don't bluster
and blow. They understand
that coercion never creates
lasting results.

Any time we sense a weakening of trust,
we need to search proactively, and immediately,
to discover its cause. Trust is essential
in organizations. Almost nothing
of value gets accomplished
without it.

I run in the path of your commands,
for you have set my heart free.

Psalm 119:32

The "power of prayer" resides
not in the one who prays,
nor in the words one uses.

Rather, it rests in the one,
true God to whom we pray and
who has promised to hear and help!

Despite the divine rights he could have claimed, our Savior came to his heavenly Father on his knees, on his face—in utter dependence— submitting fully to the Father's will.

A prayerful heart is a reverent, humble heart.

As we serve God's people, we sometimes struggle
to surrender to the Father's will for the lives
of those we serve, let alone for our own lives.
We sometimes doubt the Father's
wisdom and love.

Lord Jesus, because you said you would,
please pardon my self-reliance and fretfulness,
working in me a reverent, trusting,
prayerful heart.

Without focus and vision, passion dissolves and zeal quickly evaporates. Put another way, those who try to do everything accomplish little or nothing.

34

A stream without banks quickly grows into a very large puddle. Banks provide boundaries and make it possible for a river to flow freely and purposefully within those boundaries.

What is your life about?

What is your organization up to?

Call it a purpose. Call it a vision. Call it a preferred future state. Whatever you call it, your vision channels your energy. Your vision sets boundaries and provides focus.

Lord God, Holy Spirit, sharpen my vision,
granting me passion for your purposes.
May I serve my Servant-King with
a zealous heart, a heart on fire
with love for him and for
those he still seeks!

_____

Let us not grow weary of doing good,
for in due season we will reap, if we do not give up.
So then, as we have opportunity, let us do good
to everyone, and especially to those who are
of the household of faith.

Galatians 6:9–10 ESV

_____

The Living God. The Scriptures use this name to distinguish between the true God and all false gods. The name implies both power and willingness to act; the Living God moves on behalf of his people.

As the rain and the snow
come down from heaven,
and do not return to it
without watering the earth
and making it bud and flourish,
so that it yields seed for the sower and bread for the eater,
so is my word that goes out from my mouth:

It will not return to me empty,
but will accomplish what I desire
and achieve the purpose for which I sent it.

Isaiah 55:10–11

To know Christ.
To become like Christ.
To share Christ.

The Living Christ still acts today
on our behalf and on behalf of
those we serve in his name.
We may see results right now—or not.
We may feel we're getting somewhere—or not.
But no matter what we see or feel,
Jesus *is* at work.

We have his Word of promise!

Lord Jesus, fill my
heart with faith that holds
on to your strong promises
and continues to speak
your Word faithfully.

Jesus gives the gift of rest—even to those whose
days are filled with service to him.

How are you taking care of yourself
spiritually and physically?
When do you take time to let Christ serve *you*?

*[Jesus said,] "Come to me, all you who are
weary and burdened, and I will
give you rest."*

Matthew 11:28

Lord Jesus, open my ears to hear you calling me, whether to work or to rest. May I respond to your call with a heart filled with love and trust in you!

To cheer the downcast . . .
To caution the one who strays . . .
To comfort the one who's weary . . .

This is angels' work on earth—and we get to do it!

[The] angels are . . . spirits sent to care
for people who will inherit salvation.

Hebrews 1:14 NLT

Lord Jesus,

grant that your joy —

the joy of pardon and peace —

may strengthen my heart,

as you renew me for

today's tasks.

46

Sharing Christ's care
makes an eternal difference!

Lord God, Holy Spirit, develop in my heart an eternal perspective as I contemplate my service for the Lord Jesus, that I be ever diligent and watchful, as I work and wait for his return.

48

Only one life,
It soon will pass.
Only what's done
For Christ will last.

A Note to Our Readers . . .

If this book has made a difference in your life or if you have simply enjoyed it, we would like to hear from you. Your words would encourage us!

You can reach us at:

Editorial Department
CTA, Inc.
PO Box 1205
Fenton, MO 63026-1205

Or by e-mail at editor@CTAinc.com